Long-Haul Travellers

I came too soon to some places,
too late to many others.

— *Hávamál*, ca AD700-900

Long-Haul Travellers
Sheenagh Pugh

seren

Seren is the book imprint of
Poetry Wales Press Ltd.
57 Nolton Street, Bridgend, Wales, CF31 3AE
01656 663018
www.seren-books.com

ISBN 978-1-85411-477-8

A CIP record for this title is available from the British Library.

The publisher acknowledges the financial assistance of the Welsh Books Council.

Cover photograph: Geirangerfjorden by Michael Burns

Printed in Bembo by Bell & Bain, Glasgow

Sheenagh Pugh's website: http://sheenagh.googlepages.com

You can also see Sheenagh Pugh reading the Webcam Sonnet: 4 'Now' on UTube.
www.youtube.com/watch?v=X6JbkgzijaM - 52k

Contents

The Art of Packing

The trick is to take only
what will be scarce
where you are going.

Parry, icebound, months
from sun, surveys ship's stores
by a candle,

seeing clearly, now,
what was worth its room:
the barrel organ

crammed with song and dance,
bank holidays, trips
to pleasure beaches.

The theatre trunk: long hair,
lip-rouge, gauze scarves
drifting like scent.

But he shakes his head
over frozen chronometers,
wishing he'd used

space better; packed the dark
corners tight with daylight,
shafts filtered

through trees, warm summer
evenings. Should have squeezed in
one more sunrise.

Josephine

Never a credulous man, he liked ghost stories
the way a journalist does, investigating
with his mind made up, his instinct debunking
spectral footsteps into loose shutters,
ghost-horses into guilt, spirit-messages
into hokum.

So many times, he had lain down hoping
she would come back in dreams, and she did not.
One day, out driving, he glimpsed her face at the window
of an old house. Just grief, he told himself,
playing tricks on his eyes. He will sign the deeds
tomorrow.

His mind is full of old tales and new wonders:
a house that grants wishes, a woman who wills
her lover's illness into her own body,
a man who drives to a wood of dead bluebells
where bereaved parents walk hand in hand
with children.

The dead come so far. They negotiate,
lopsided with baggage, so many customs posts,
doubtful officials, time zones, to stand on your doorstep
washed out, with the patience of long-haul travellers
in their eyes. When they call, it seems polite
to be in.

Hundreds of Ships

i.m. George Mackay Brown

They say it's the long winter that leans its weight
on the heart; the drone of wind that interferes
with the tuning. And they say it's ingrained:
there was an uncle, haunted by the masts
of sunken ships in the harbour; only he
could see them, that forest of raised arms
waving for help, until one day he went
himself to see what they wanted.

And you too might have gone down, an ocean
in your lungs, and nothing against the cold
but an afterglow of whisky. Except you found
a way up, a rope of words into the air.
Dying, you said, "I see hundreds and hundreds of ships
going out of the harbour," and all the luckless wrecks
surfaced and turned to little paper boats
on their way round the world, unsinkable.

A Dream of Leningrad

He is visiting Leningrad – which has never
had another name – for the second time,

and he is troubled, feels he should recall
more than he does. The city is granite and marble;

he senses great height, though bizarrely
each detailed stone finial is up close,

at eye level. Or *he* is up close, high
above streets and bridges, looking down

like God. It all reminds him of Manchester
for no reason he can get a grip on,

though when they find themselves in the suburbs
the red brick is Derby to the life,

and further out, the white mansions of the rich
have a look of Lego. He should be able to guide

his fellow travellers, should be slipping
the city back on like an old coat,

knowing what's round each corner, but the feel
eludes him. Only once, on the outskirts,

on a long road of factory outlets,
does some nondescript petrol station

touch off a memory, and the city
he is leaving rushes back on him,

the sense of loss so aching, so perfect,
it wakes him, to spend the day wondering

where, since he never set eyes on Leningrad,
never left it, never had it to lose,

this grief comes from, that is as real
as the flagstones under his feet.

Adwaitya

died Calcutta, 2006, estimated age 250

I understand their sounds
– how not, after so long?
But I have

no answers. They lean over
my fence, throw greens
and questions, as if

I could reply.
"Were you really Clive's tortoise?"
I beam

short-sightedly. I've no idea.
There have been many hands
proffering lettuce,

many blurred faces
high above. I do recall one:
sad voice, sad eyes,

who would watch me munch
for hours. At the time, I thought
it eased his mind,

but they say he stopped
his life in the end.
Such little lives

as they have; you would think
there was no time
to tire of them.

After I knew
they did not last, I took
less note. I have watched

young grow old, their years
racing like days, and then
they stop. I view them now

as purveyors of leaves
and bran. I am partial to bran.
But getting to know

one from another seems futile
for so short a time.
They marvel

to see me amble, chew.
That I still am,
after so long, like trees

or stones, gives them
some comfort.
Lately, even bran

has lost its taste. I think
I may stop soon,
and I fear for them,

their sad eyes
seeing change
where they looked for certainty.

Golden Boy

25 November 2005

A white day
to go: November slipping
away underfoot,

rusting
or jaundiced, brittle with frost.
Your face,

fine-boned
even now, not drowned in flesh,
but turned to gold,

skin beaten out
to the thinnest leaf,
a god's mask,

if gods could die
or come to grief. That sheen,
as if death

refined you,
burned off the slag, left only
the right metal,

unalloyed,
the flash of talent, the joy
speeding and weaving

to its goal,
baffling all challenge, laughing
at its gift.

We grow up:
put away childish things, stop
hoping for fame

or genius,
same as the rest. But just
now and then,

a man rises
above everyday, a man
like us,

and we fly
a little way on his uplift.
What if

he comes down
in the end to ruin?
It is the brief

instant aloft,
the leaving earth, that lives,
as when a boy,

falling,
still glowed from having once
touched the sun.

The Boyhood of Tristan Jones

By the shore, it might be,

        he would stare at shapes

shifting in the shallows,

        filling with sea,

pulsing like heartbeats.

        Purple veins

trembled, suspended

        in the vague translucence

that passed for a body.

        They seemed beings

without bounds, or rather

        whose bounds were fixed

by their own fancy.

Later he would find them

        left by the ebb,

cauls of radiance

        capping the rocks.

Sun-dried, they thinned

        to a mere membrane,

an iridescent glaze,

        as if they wished

to colour stone different,

        yet leave themselves

open to debate,

        outlines to be hatched,

made up, narrated.

Interviewing the Two Last Speakers

The young researcher, in at the death,
can't credit his luck. A language,

a whole language, passing out of use,
out of knowledge, unless he can catch

each mumbled word of these old women
as it falls, and fix it in print,

where it will forget how to elude
definition, change colour, grow

new subtleties. He's sad for the words,
pinned down on paper, but he thrills

to hear them spoken. His fingers
cramp, trying to keep up: *goodbye*

*is gendered; come rhymes with go
and nothing declines in the plural.*

Two columns in his notebook: two
old women giving him words,

the two last speakers. Often
they differ; an accent will shift

the word's shape, a memory
turn a meaning. In his riches

he longs for more: a conversation,
words picked up, sent back, two voices

fusing or sparking. It can't be,
he knows: the two last speakers,

loathing each other, have not met
or talked in years. This speech will never

again be current, a conduit
for thought, anger, wit. He takes notes

while there's still time: *the verb
to lose has no present tense.*

Paul Hunter at the Welsh Open, 1996

He was seventeen; he brought it alive,
the tournament full of jaded men

twice his age, who'd stopped having fun.
Rows of old ladies were going *aaahhh*

whenever he flicked back his long hair.
He kept the crowd buzzing, made them laugh,

and the cameras could none of them get enough,
all day, of his smile. *One to remember,*

said the commentators, spying the future.
He was the talk, the next thing coming,

the sport's new face; he was young and winning
and finding it easy; his talent gleamed

like the gold his fingers carelessly combed.
That day, he had ten years to live.

The Opportune Moment

"If you were waiting for the opportune moment, that was it"
– Capt. Jack Sparrow, *Pirates of the Caribbean; Curse of the Black Pearl*

When you go ashore in that town,
take neither a camera nor a notebook.
However many photographs you upload
of that street, the smell of almond paste
will be missing; the harbour will not sound
of wind slapping on chains. You will read
notes like "Sami church", later, and know
you saw nothing, never put it where
you could find it again, were never
really there. When you go ashore
in the small port with the rusty trawlers,
there will be fur hawkers who all look
like Genghis Khan on a market stall,
crumbling pavements, roses frozen in bud,
an altar with wool hangings, vessels
like canal ware, a Madonna
with a Russian doll face. When you go
ashore, take nothing but the knowledge
that where you are, you never will be again.

Leaving

She has grandchildren at home; she texts them
now and again, when the daylight fails,

but mostly she's at the forward rail
looking out for the new, the next port,

where she will walk down every street
she can fit into the time. Always last

up the gangplank; whoever wastes
a minute of the journey, it won't be her.

Leaving port, she stays aft, looking back longer
than anyone at yet another place

she'll never see again. For years, her days
have been full of goodbyes. You'd think sailing

away would pall. She shakes her head, smiling.
"Oh, but it gets easier each time."

The Girl Taken By An Eagle

Sometimes I think it must have reeked of meat
like a butcher's in summer, a foul breath
on the back of my neck. I can fancy
feeling cold in the shadow of its wings.
But the truth is, I recall nothing.

The way I always heard it told,
I was playing outside; my mother turned
her back a moment, and I was gone.
She saw our neighbours staring upward,
mouths agape, followed their gaze and screamed.

Everyone screamed, hoping to frighten it
into dropping me, until it flew
so high, they dared not. In all the din
I made no sound that they could hear.
Like enough, I took it for a game –

I was three, after all. When it dropped me
on the rock, a shout went up, and the lads,
the nest-robbers whose mothers never guessed
how high they ventured, came climbing after.
And one, the most daring, gained the ledge,

as everyone knows, and brought me down.
I heard it all the time: on birthdays,
at school, when I met someone new.
It was like a tale that had happened
to someone else, some princess in a book.

Of course, the brave lad should have got
the princess and half the kingdom,
which he didn't. But I did marry,
had children, still live, after seventy years,
in sight of the island where I was born,

where it happened. If. Now comes this fellow,
says it never did, that no eagle
could have done it. He thinks I climbed there
myself; he even brought a child
to show it could be done.

What then of all the memories?
People saw an eagle in the sky,
a child on a mountain ledge, mistook them
for part of the same tale? My mother
always swore she saw it carry me.

But tales grow in the telling. I should know.
I used to look at eagles and think,
if only I'd known *that* was as high and far
as ever my life would reach, I'd have taken
more notice at the time.

No-one knows the moments that will matter,
not at the time, not when they're happening.
That was mine, on the ledge, that made me
The Girl Who Was Taken By An Eagle,
which I have been all my life,

wishing I could recall it. Now it seems,
after all, I was in the wrong story.
The Girl Who Climbed A Mountain – she sounds
bolder, more fun. Maybe I should have been her,
if I'd known. If you ever know.

Seafarers' Memorial, Trondheim

They could be father and son, so together,
though the older man, cold, huddled

in his greatcoat, is looking straight ahead,
his mind bent on where he is bound.

The boy's eyes wander, as if no end
were yet fixed to his journey. His shirt open

to the waist, he might be the man
he walks beside, twenty years ago,

a summer ghost, or a rueful echo
of men who were young when he was young

and who now will never age, never bring
their kitbags home, nor read the words cut

on the plinth, beneath their stone boots:
Many ships and seamen never come to harbour.

A True Story

Peder Olsen Feidie wrote a poem
in the leper hospital at Bergen,

and it was not a great poem.
Critics would have called it unformed;

words like conventional, anecdotal,
simplistic, would have been freely used.

It told of the life he once had,
playing at home, like any small boy,

until his skin thickened and dried out
so hard, he could feel neither heat nor cold,

nerves dead, the muscles in his face
too paralysed to smile. It told how,

one day, he saw his mother look at him
in a new way: *my burden,* not *my son.*

It told of years in the hospital:
work, treatment, mealtimes, every day

the same, of sores and ulcers, claw hands
and lost toes. It told how, in the chapel,

he recoiled from the darkness of his thoughts,
uglier, he believed, than his body,

and how he comforted himself
with the distant promise of death,

and it was not a great poem:
it didn't need to be.

Vardø Fort

A perfect star shaped in stone and turf,
pretty and intimate as a dolls' house.

Furnished rooms, plates ready for use,
as if the garrison were not long gone.

Tourists posing by the lone rowan
that needs wrapping against salt arctic air.

Whitewashed walls built by slave prisoners,
the low beam where once, a visiting king

cracked his head. Officers froze, fearing
his anger, but he just laughed, borrowed

a knife, carved his name into the wood
and went his way; he was a jovial soul

and a busy one, on a mission to heal
his nation, and witches don't burn themselves.

Murat Reis

That city: brick, grey stone.
When the wind was right,

it breathed the sweetness
of brewery malt.

Each winter, canals froze
under heavy linen skies;

boys' skates scribbled
grisaille on the ice.

A street brazier's red
warmed his hands, stung his eyes.

***

His name is Janszoon, Jansen, Jansz, perhaps;
could be from Haarlem, could be forty-four.

What's certain: he's a Dutch privateer
licensed to harry Spain, which he does well.

Then he vanishes, as a coastline will
in sudden fog, so the helmsman must write

his map from memory on the blank white.
When the fog lifts, it is on a new place.

The name: Morad, Morato, Murat Reis:
he plunders merchantmen, trades prisoners,

Christian slaves out of Europe to Algiers.
He flies the blood-red flag of Barbary,

unless the prey are Spanish; they will see
orange colours on his closing ships.

***

The first thing slaves learn

      there are no rules

that work all the time.

      He entertains captives

now and then in his cabin

      conversing civilly

watching them

      read his moods like weather.

When he smokes on deck

      at ease in silk cushions

and they eye him sideways

      he feels them looking

at their burned houses.

      Sometimes he gives them

a smile in passing

      to see their faces

slacken with relief.

      It is good practice

for when they are sold

      and their lives centre

on one man as arbitrary

      as the god who left them.

In a few days more

      they will fetch Algiers

where their story may take them

      to a galley bench

or favour and freedom

      like any folk tale.

If his own story

      were written in his face

it might comfort them

      or maybe not.

You live now he tells them

      in a new world.

★★★

Safe under treaty, Murat Reis
victuals at a Dutch port.
Some sight he is,

embroidered silk, gold thread
lighting a grey day.
The harbourmaster's look

would freeze milk, but boys
on the quay gaze out,
sick with envy.

Jan Janszoon's wife, come
from Haarlem, holds a small
wide-eyed girl by the hand

and calls her man home.
Murat Reis stares
past her through the rain

until she turns and walks
away, the child, looking back,
dragging on her arm.

★★★

Englishmen, not getting the hang
of foreign speech, call him *Matthew Rice*:

it amuses him to hear stories
of Matthew the English renegade

from men who know his home town, his trade,
who'll tell how they sailed with him one summer.

Murat Reis smiles; if he didn't know better,
he might almost believe in the man.

And what's another name? The first one,
the family name, the one you can lose,

that matters. Drop that, and you can use
any one you want, like flags and gods.

He never sets them right; it makes no odds,
and maybe one day they won't be wrong.

★★★

This city: green
floating above white,

a dazzle of lime-bleached stone
roofed with gardens.

The wind smells of orange trees;
it brings him heat,

a plash of small fountains,
camels coughing, percussion

from a thousand slave chains,
a call to prayer.

★★★

He wonders about women

                how used they are

to change their names

           fit themselves

into new families

              sleep with the enemy.

He has known a woman

                captured in Iceland

fluent in Arabic

            when they reached Algiers.

They flow like that

                    put on new colours

like creatures he has seen

               shifting in the deep

changing shape

          with each tide's pulse.

All over Algiers

                in parks and markets

fair-skinned hands reach out

                  from cloaks to catch

at olive children

          veiled voices scolding

in local words

            and northern accents.

Is it all from fear

        a sense of fate

or are they so made

           they revel in the chance

to refashion themselves

              start a new life?

The way his Moroccan woman

                his sons' mother

echoes his gutturals

        sings soft-voiced

a Dutch lullaby

       a pirate ballad.

Such fluidity

      he thinks in the end

may be a way

      of staying the same.

★★★

No choice without some holding back.
He had his chances to go home.

Lying, iced-in, off Amsterdam,
he saw land close: did not jump ship.

Captured by Christians, he passed up
the Church's bait of glad recall

for one turned Turk against his will.
He paid his ransom and made straight

for the white harbour, Moorish light,
his sons, his castle. Now and then

the light feels flat. That moment when
he'd wake in autumn, breathing knives,

and know the frost was in the leaves:
years now, his throat has missed that ache.

★★★

In the castle where Murat Reis,
home from the sea,
passes the last of his days,

there is great to-do
for a guest, a young woman
in foreign dress,

bare-faced, with wide grey eyes
that look long
at everything: latticed light

patterning the silk cushions,
the glowing carpet,
the face of Murat Reis

streaked silver with tears
like her own. Lysbeth Janszoon
van Haarlem spends a summer

in the palace by the shore,
then leaves for home
without looking back.

***

The sons of Murat Reis,
restless in Morocco,
sail to the New World.

Anthony Jansen van Salee
farms Manhattan, prospers,
quarrels with his neighbours,

owns a deep anchorage
where strange ships berth,
showing no colours.

They call him *the Turk*
for his dark face;
he leaves his children

a book whose script flows,
but baffles them all,
knowing no Arabic.

This is many years
after Murat Reis,
one day in Algiers

at the crest of fortune,
cajoled a consul
for an English passport,

gripping his shoulder, whispering
urgently, *I was ever
a Christian at heart.*

Fame

At the funeral of the great hero
the whole army stood for hours,
getting heatstroke, while each commander
spoke his praise, including those
who never liked him. His armour
glittered in the sun: the High King
eyed it uneasily, foreseeing trouble
when the will was read. The deceased's mother,
a minor goddess, lit the pyre
and a fortune in aromatic gums
went up in sweet, dizzying smoke,
while the soldiers, heads throbbing, choked
their nausea back. The hero's horse,
a couple of hounds and some prisoners
were added, throats slit, to the flames
and folk went back to their business.

Now, at dusk, slaves slip out,
a day's work in their slumped shoulders,
aching for bed. No-one notices
as they trudge, without a glance,
past the pyre of the great hero,
clutching locks of hair, hacked off
with kitchen knives, to lay
on the slowly greening mound
they tend for Patroklos, who always
spoke to them kindly.

Regina

Arbeia: "fort of the Arab troops"

Cold is what they will notice
first, this company,

Syrians from the Tigris,
landed on the Tyne.

The commander will take
one look, fish out his cloak

and have a new house built,
underfloor heating throughout.

His troops, every chance, will haunt
the baths, lap up

steam, swap memories
of warm summer nights.

Barates of Palmyra,
finding his bed cold,

will buy a woman
of the Cattivellauni,

free her, marry her,
name her Regina.

She'll hold to the light
the brooch he bought her,

listen, smiling,
to his tales of deserts,

fig trees, shaded gardens.
When, aged thirty

for ever, she is figured
in stone, the east wind

and the river mist
will chill Barates

less than his suddenly
ungoverned house.

Victor

Arbeia Fort, South Shields

He is shown reclining, being served:
we are to know he was a gentleman,
no menial. His dignity is carved
in each fold of cloth, each word on the stone.
To Victor among the shades: by nation
a Moor, a freedman, though once slave
to Numerianus of the First Asturian,
who with all love attended him to the grave.

And the XX: such a short way to write
twenty years… So proud, enthroned above
his tiny cupbearer; so fortunate,
the glow of triumph on him, this rising star
who'd won his freedom and his master's love,
wearing his youth like armour. Ave, Victor.

Absent

They're everywhere, the absent. You go
out walking and see a young man
with the slight stoop and long, loping stride
of the very tall, and you have almost hailed
your son before you know it is some stranger,
some other son whose doppelganger, no doubt,
is duping his mother on a distant street.

And in the supermarket aisle you slow
to a near-stop, following old men
whose heads are mottled, whose white hair strays,
shining, on their collars, and none of them
is your father, though when one stumbles,
your hands steady him in the same moment,
as if they had been always in readiness.

You used to think death made a difference:
your mother, no longer censuring on the phone
or face to face, has long been missing
even from your dreams, nor do you meet her
drifting down some street she never saw.
Yet she too waits in ambush, in shop glass
or a sudden mirror, there before you know it.

Mr Sahara

At birth, like every boy of the Wodaabe,
he was given his own mirror.

All through childhood his teeth were bleached,
his limbs stretched into elegance.

A lovely boy is his family's fortune.
He could be crowned Mr Sahara,

please the panel of female judges,
make a good marriage.... Tonight

should be his big night. He's sleeked
and groomed, painted with the clays

he walked miles to find. He glances,
as he was taught, from under his eyelashes

up at the ladies, his smile
hesitant. They read it as shyness,

approvingly. But he's wondering
if the woman who takes him will still be kind

when his looks fade. Watching his sisters,
mirrorless, unconscious of the faces

they never see, it has crossed his mind
to guess at how free that feels.

Knitting Silver

Fine silver wire
cast on like wool,

hurting. The jeweller's
cut fingers

plain-purl a fall
of flashing mesh,

knitting her country
between the needles.

Veins of gneiss
and serpentine glinting

in the rock, fishing-nets
lifting from the ocean,

sieving light. Grey pleats
in the silk of a loch,

the backlit cirrus
of a mackerel sky.

A drop of blood
spots the polished helix

of herring, chain-links
wheeling as one,

their mercury pattern
Mexican-waving

through time and water
to the netted moment.

Saxa Vord

The hill hides as hills do
behind bends, dips in the road, houses;

until some angle conjures it back,
its zigzag path climbing into cloud.

When the crest clears, there is no castle,
no high window, no golden rope.

There is a dome, a bluish shadow
flanked by thin spires: Taj Mahal

in the far north. This hill was once
forbidden, to all but its guards.

Now gates gape: only steepness
for a barrier. It is not so far,

even on foot, the road no cars take now
past green lower slopes, past the firth

opening out, past upland moors where skuas
dive-bomb intruders, coming in fast

at head height, the only guards left.
At the road's end, a locked gate

in a perimeter fence whose wire knitting
unravels daily, sheep-breached, posts

falling back, radiation warnings
fading and tarnished. Who knows if they're true,

or just one last line of defence?
This was a listening post; up close

its spires are spider-webbed with cables
to catch movement. Speed, altitude, direction

vibrated down their filaments. The great dome
squatted in its network, not blue after all

but dark brown. Now, already, paint
peels from its lightless facets.

It sensed whatever stirred in the air,
the whisper of a threat. Who knows

if those were real? They seemed so, at the time,
and the guards on the northernmost rock

could look back, on a bright day,
over miles of hills, fields, strands

glinting white, the intricate coastline
of islands, hundreds, unfolding

southward, beyond their sight,
but in their lee. They knew themselves

sentinels, always looking outward
beyond the pale, across an ocean

the wind shivered into green and purple,
as once it shaped waves of grass

above Housesteads, when the lads
looked out from the Wall.

One day, someone looks out and admits
the enemy is not coming;

he has changed his ways, or maybe
he was never there at all,

and new orders come round. Some folk
move on; some, stayed by love,

turn their hand to other trades,
as they can. But a fort, unpurposed,

falls into ruin. Old walls,
fragmenting, haunt the fancy;

we are less used to find romance
in wire and concrete. Yet this,

posed to see and be seen
on its high bluff, had attitude

enough for any broch.
It held secrets, dangers, intimacies;

it was an outpost, a fellowship
on the edge; it was Ultima Thule.

And it is as empty now,
as eloquent of absence,

as any deserted village
or unroofed hall, any space

where company was, and speech,
and work going forward.

So long listening out,
tracking, recording

everything but themselves,
their voices, their steps, the moments

they made here. Under the wind
and the jeering seabirds

there is a word-shaped silence,
and on one office wall

an outside light
shining through the day,

as if the last man
forgot to turn it off.

Exact Language

We need a word for this slow drifting
free of people, the way it comes
not to matter if you never see them.
All the exact languages are dying,
the ones with words like *pirr, Shetlandic:*
a light breeze on a summer's day.
Whid, Scottish: to move as fluidly
as an unstartled hare. Where are our words
for the plainsong of massed wind turbines
or a man who outlives all his friends?
Which verb means to feel grief
for the death of someone who never lived?
What language has no need of *onsra,*
Boro: to love for the last time?

Bioluminescent

Do we seem simple, such beings
scarcely other than ocean

held in bubbles, pulsating
fingerbreadths of Atlantic,

conduits for food and water
that rush through, hardly pausing

or changing? Yet we shape language
out of light. Our fluent skin

floods with the shades of mating,
disguise, escape. We can silver

ourselves, mirror the world
and disappear. If danger

touches us, we convulse
into spasms of radiance,

colours that shout to summon
the killers of our killers.

Is it true that your skins
are all but dumb,

can stammer no more than a brief
pallor, a momentary flush?

Missing Fire

Remember, Odin, the old days
when we mixed our blood.
          —Loki: *The Poetic Edda*

When the earth shakes, I know
you are in pain,

and I think how you came
out of the world's morning
calling me cousin, eyes alight
with mischief.
                I pressed our wrists
close, blending the blood.

It was a time of flux,
new against old, us
against them. Your wits sparked
like flame off flint,
and you used them for us.

Our enemies are slow
but lasting: stone grinds down
blade. But we gave them a run
back then: God, we did.
You scheming, scamming our way
past the puzzled troll-face
of evil, your eyes
laughing into mine.

Me defending you
to the godly, who stayed pure
while you broke oaths
to save them. They never
quite trusted you. If you tricked
the dark, it was for love
of trickery, not of us.
                        I knew.
I didn't care, warming
my hands at your joy.

You and me, so alike
we might have been brothers.
Shape-shifters both, turning words
wrong way out, cozeners
and guizers, we made ourselves up
like stories. But you outdid
my dreams. Little white mare,
I ride your foal.

The ground you suffer under
is torn and bleeding.

Your lips were scarred,
twisted, where you ripped out
the stitches of the righteous.
My reprobate,
I'd have unpicked them
so gently, you'd have felt nothing.

It grew slowly,
the dark inside you.
There was no one day
fun soured into malice.
There was a day
I had to look
at a face whose eyes
blazed hate, whose tongue
kindled feuds, lit slanders,
who had been you.
                        Oh my fire,
they say, if you stare
long enough into flame,
you go blind.

Among the children of light
I miss the brightness
that is danger, the glint
of wolf-eye, serpent-scale.
The wolf in you,
whose fur has flown up
electric under my hand,
will kill me one day.

In the Moment

It's nothing personal, this way
he has of moving on,

not looking back. The visits
he will not pay to towns

he lived in, the letters
he doesn't write

to ex-neighbours. How names
can't seem to stay

in mind, once he no longer
uses them. How he could never

see his mother's face
in dreams, after she died.

How he lives
in the moment, focusing

on a vapour trail, a ripple,
a held note. Keeping

no diary, no camera.
A long time since

he looked at a photograph,
seeing the day, failing

to call it back, to feel
what he tried to frame.

Camera Obscura

Edinburgh 1874

High in the tower there is a room
and in this room there is no light
but from a vast white shallow bowl,
and round its rim the people watch
a woman outlined on the dark,
holding a shaft that reaches up
into the roof, to the great lens.

They are unsure what they will see,
but open to enlightenment,
as this city has always been,
letting the gleam of the pale face
guide them in shadow, trusting her
to show them how the magic works,
the reason in the world's wonder.

With a cupped hand under the shaft
she guides it, then lets go and spills
the whole city into her bowl,
a map where shoppers stroll the Mile
and traffic moves, outside the tower
and in the room, no conjuror's trick,
but happening, and here and now.

She rests a hand inside the bowl
and lets one little figure walk
on to her palm, then closes him
inside a fist, and all around
breath is drawn in with a soft hiss
as the hand rises, opens up
to show not the least smear of blood,

and then she smiles and makes them look
back at the bowl, where still he walks,
never once dreaming he was taken
out of the world, into a hand
he cannot see. The show being done,
they edge away, dismissed, eyeing
the city sky with some unease.

The Pause

It was like a huge intake
of air, that moment
when the sea drew back

and held a breath
that stretched out
for ever, a pause

into which you could whisper
a word, and change
the world.

It was like the moment
much later,
in the wave's wake,

when the embassy clerk,
resolving chaos,
asked him his name,

and in the pause
he saw himself
a man without papers,

marking time
in a foreign land,
a man whose family

would think him dead.
His debts cancelled,
his choices all

to make again,
he held back,
drawing out the while

between past and future
before opening
his mouth in a lie.

Newport

How many times – hundreds? – has he seen
the Usk at ebb, slug-trailing between mudbanks
gross and rubbery as the obese
naked flanks of some sea-mammal;
how often has he suffered that grey,
tidemarked with ringpulls and till receipts,
leaching into the sky, the town, his life,
all stranded, all going nowhere.

But what he knows is the one time,
tide not long out, sun shivering
off wet, the banks were silver, so much light
it hurt. Usk in arms, pennants of paper
brave on bright metal, the true journey
happening always, as real as what you see.

Webcam Sonnets

1. Knowing

On the webcam the wet street gleams,
morning-shadowed, flowing to the harbour;

if you didn't know, you would see a river.
A mast rises through the half-light:

the Market Cross. Its lantern picks out
the pilot boat's empty berth; they must be bringing

a ship in. You look at everything
and see beyond it to what you know.

This place like home, so ingrained in you,
how can it still go about its life

in your absence? In your mind it's as if
they pack it away every time you leave,

yet here it is, loved, impervious to love,
called by a touch, unreachable through a screen.

2. Voyeur

When the cam refreshes, a warehouse window
has turned into a point of white light;

by the next thirty-second update
it's a blinding disc. You think *explosion*

and *what can I do* and *nothing. Watch it happen.*
The seconds count down; your gut tenses.

You breathe in at the change, see radiance
welling out over half the screen. *Beautiful.*

Not beautiful. There might be people:
if you keep looking, you might see them die.

But you keep looking. And when, blessedly,
the update shows, after all, sun dazzling

off glass, no worse, it doesn't leave you feeling
much better. You know what you would do.

3. Contact

A man stands at a prearranged time
in a certain spot, smiling fixedly

towards a camera he can't see,
mobile ringing close to his ear.

A woman answers, takes her phone over
to a screen. *I'm clicking in Favourites*

but it's taking for ever to load the site,
stay where you are, don't move… Oh,

I can see you now. I can see you.
The small, fuzzy picture shows a place

halfway across the world, and there he is,
in his blue shirt, at this very moment,

not seeing her. She cannot speak, intent
on his blurred face, hardly hearing him.

4. Now

Film and photograph only show
how it was. You're seeing how it is,

now, this moment. A moody sunrise
bruising the nimbus above Hammerfest

to a nacreous flush that will never outlast
the next refresh. The very townsfolk

will miss it, unless they chance to look
now, right now. Can you catch his attention,

the man crossing the Torg, head down;
can you make him see one moment of sky

unlike all the others you and he
will walk under today, unlike the moment

passing in Padua, Jaipur, Tashkent,
that you don't happen to be watching now?

The Door to the Sea

If the stiff door stood open,
the arch in the stone

would be framed in thorns,
ivy, twisted boughs,

and beyond, a lawn: mole-hills
leading to a gate

that gives on to a footpath
you can follow

over the field, between tussocks
and cowpats, then down

a lane overgrown
with brambles, all the way

to the wide hem of the world,
beaded with light,

the distant edge on which
all doors should open.

Translation

After Tom Anderson's air, 'Da Slokkit Light'

What he sees: the peninsula,
his childhood's map open
before him, and it is night.
He pauses on the hill.

Lights come on in homesteads
all over the headland; he knows
each cluster, the constellations
of Braehoulland, Solheim, Easthouse.

What else he sees: the spaces.
Across empty tracts of black
he traces the patterns
of all the missing stars

that now prickle only
at the back of his eyes,
their names no longer
known to the postman.

What he can do: translate
darkened windows, lost friends
into music. Grief reaches upwards
and falls back, in an air

that holds on to each sound,
desperately, until
a little row of stopped notes
dropping, one by one, into the dark.

Signature

The elderly casualty in A & E
was carrying no papers when he stepped
absent-mindedly in front of a tram.

His face, bearded, commonplace, unconscious,
did not give the busy nurses pause,
did not put them in mind of palm trees

petrified into columns, or façades
where scooped balconies clung like martins' nests
and never a wall rose straight. The buildings

they passed coming to work. He lay still,
giving no trouble, not looking at all
like a man who'd ice a roof, as if

houses belonged in fairy tales, who'd talk
one patron into bankrolling a park
full of follies, and another into waiting

a century. *My client is in no hurry.*
He slipped away, as they say, in the end,
unsuspected, still waiting for a name,

the man who'd signed a city. A body
decently laid out on a bed,
eighteen improbable towers on his mind.

Legendary Lover

Boys in the classroom
texted their love;

she felt the phone buzz,
an undertone

of constant passion
in her hip pocket,

too quiet
for Sir's ageing ears,

and she smiled, but chose
the one who took trouble

to write out in full
his worship, shape it

into a dart
and aim it home.

The Muralist

He was master of his trade:
many a drab gable-end
coloured at his touch.

Figures came to life firing,
crouched in ambush, rising, arms back,
to hurl grenades.

Yet he'd a taste for the fancy,
could adorn a capital U
like any monk.

These new days, he's in demand
to paint over the past.
No more red hands.

He's fine with rainbows, sunbursts;
his father's pigeons model
for peace doves.

Children are caught mid-pass
or taking a shot
at goal. But from behind.

His secret: all those years,
eyes staring from balaclavas,
he can't do faces.

Prentice again, he's learning
the play of mood across features,
sun on a plain,

getting the hang of writing
stories on skin, the way
a smile works.

Men of Iron

Anthony Gormley's 'Another Place':
Crosby Beach, July 2005

Land at his back, he scans
the beach, the breaking surf

where, ankle-deep, his likeness
mirrors his stance, staring

at his own double, immersed
up to the waist, eyes fixed

far out, on a dark head
showing above the waves.

All along the bay's curve,
between high-water mark

and low, a hundred cast-iron clones
stand, paddle, wade;

you would not know them
from us, at a distance,

until sun sets and the beach
empties, and they wait

still, as the slap and suck
of tide on gleaming sand

ebbs from their feet. They bear
the day's decorations,

handkerchiefs knotted on their heads,
genitals spray-painted,

and the rust's graffiti
spreading like a bruise,

while they, enduring,
keep watch for the ones

further out, the spaces
where no heads show.

Come November
they will be gone,

and folk who know
they are in New York

will still be narrowing
their gaze, as if a keen eye

might catch the last of them
walking out to sea.

Fixed

Anthony Gormley's 'Another Place':
Crosby Beach, April 2007

Built on sand, anchored
for good, they gaze out

west across the sea
where they should have gone.

Born to be travellers,
they have left gaps

in the skylines of Cuxhaven,
De Panne, Stavanger,

where folk came to know them,
then let them go.

Now, on this beach
like any other,

words like *home* and *always*
ambush them, pin them down.

They should have unpacked
in New York, but love

holds them back, demanding
no less than possession,

cancelling their passports,
giving them a space

to call their own, whose guesthouse
was the world. Suffering

attention like some pet animal,
fond hands stroking their flanks,

they stare past love, eyes
fixed on distance.

The Unconversations

He murmurs "Atkinson Terrace" or "Chinese crackers"
and she laughs softly, decoding at once
the shared references that baffle outsiders.

She will leave off halfway through a sentence;
he could finish it, if he felt the need.
Sometimes a gesture or a glance will do.

The longer the marriage, the more goes unsaid:
too much at stake for him to tell her now
that she cooks badly; that her snoring wakes him,

and she won't be mentioning her black tulip
missing from its bed, snapped off the stem
for a girl she cuts dead. Things to keep:

secrets, accounts, going, pretences up,
anything you've had a long time.

What It Means

such a one-minute-alive prism–
splintering silvershivering spasm
flailing on deck hook out flung
in a bucket tail slapping
the side frantic
                        slower
                                    quiet
and look now
                        the eye's surface matt
shah mat
                slack muscle
                                    scales that shed
no light
            the meaning of a word.

Grounded

Head down
against the wind, he scanned

the ground under his feet
for rabbit-holes, tussocks,

hidden burns. And tasselled grass,
wheaten-pale, shivered crazily

into surf, lit by the blue
glint of sheep's-bit, wavering

like a heat-haze, mesmerising
his gaze, until he felt

the earth shift, scudding away
beneath him as he stood

as if on cirrus, as if he
were the one thing immobile,

fixed in a stream of flying,
glittering, passing moments.

Acknowledgements

Some of these poems have previously appeared in *Acumen, Fin, Hand Luggage Only: the anthology of the Open Poetry 2007 International Sonnet Competition, Moment of Earth: Poems and Essays in Honour of Jeremy Hooker, Celtic Studies Publications, Orbis, PN Review, Poetry Review, Poetry Scotland, Poetry Wales, Seam, The Arvon Competition Anthology 2004, The New Shetlander, The North, The Peterloo Poetry Competition Anthology 2008.*

Also by the Author

Poetry:
Beware Falling Tortoises
Prisoners of Transience
Sing for the Taxman
Id's Hospit
Stonelight
The Beautiful Lie
The Movement of Bodies
Selected Poems

Fiction:
Folk Music
Kirstie's Witnesses

Non-Fiction:
The Democratic Genre: Fan fiction in a literary context